NUTS
& SEEDS

THE GOODNESS OF

NUTS & SEEDS

40 DELICIOUS NUTRITIOUS RECIPES

NATALIE SELDON

PHOTOGRAPHY BY FAITH MASON

KYLE BOOKS

CONTENTS

IN A NUTSHELL

The wellness trend has brought humble nuts and seeds into the gourmet limelight—and rightly so! Their gratifying versatility and addictive richness lend themselves to a myriad of both savory and sweet dishes.

Nuts and seeds hide many talents under their skins, providing an excellent source of nutrients and minerals. They are also gluten-, wheat- and dairy-free, making them ideal for those with intolerances or who choose to follow a vegan or paleo diet.

These pantry heroes can be blended into a smoothie to add deeper flavor, sprinkled whole on salads for all-important texture and crunch, or finely ground for a nutritious take on a tart crust. They add moisture to baked goods such as muffins and brownies, improving their keeping quality and the tenderness of crumb, and if they are toasted before grinding (one of my favorite kitchen aromas), their golden, rich nuttiness will be even more distinct. Let's celebrate these miniature powerhouses with a collection of nutritious, flavorful recipes that will inspire and bring enjoyment to the kitchen.

NUTS

SUPER NUTS & SEEDS

Nuts and seeds are a nutritional force wrapped up in a very small package. They provide generous amounts of calories, fats, complex carbohydrates, protein, and fiber, as well as proving their worth as the ultimate brain food, supplying B vitamins, omega-3s, iron, magnesium, and zinc. The phytochemicals in nuts and seeds that help fight illness include ellagic acid, flavonoids, phenolic compounds, luteolin, and isoflavones, and nuts also contain plant sterols, thought to help keep cholesterol levels in check and reduce cancer risk.

Here are some of the most popular, along with their specific health benefits:

Almonds

These can be eaten raw, roasted, or ground to make almond butter, milk, or flour. They can also be baked, used as a twist on a crumble (see page 33) or added to stir-fries and even tacos (see page 86). A wonderful source of vitamin E, which is important for a strong immune system and skin health, they also provide protein, copper, and magnesium to combat stress and promote relaxation. Almond flour is far more nutritious than wheat flours or other gluten-free flours and has a much higher fiber content.

Cashews

Actually seeds that grow at the base of cashew apples, cashews contain more iron than any other nut. Like all nuts and seeds, they are ranked highly for their healthy, heart-friendly monounsaturated fats, which help to increase good cholesterol in the blood. Packed full of soluble dietary fiber, they provide an abundant source of essential vitamins, minerals, and antioxidants. Along with macadamia nuts, they create the creamiest of nut milks and butters, and they're also popular in smoothies and creamy desserts.

Hazelnuts

Sweet-flavored nuts that can be enjoyed in an endless variety of dishes, hazelnuts have a high vitamin E content and are a good source of copper, folate, and manganese. They are also rich in antioxidants and fiber, especially when the skins are left on.

Walnuts

Recognized since ancient times as the symbol of intellectuality, walnuts are plentiful in omega-3s, which support brain and heart health, as well as ellagic acid, which aids immune function. They are also a rich source of magnesium, copper, and protein.

Pine nuts

Crunchy yet buttery in texture, pine nuts are a very good source of nutrients, essential minerals, vitamins, and heart-friendly monounsaturated fatty acids that help reduce cholesterol levels in the blood. They're delicious, especially when toasted or used in a nut crust (see page 23).

SEEDS

Pumpkin
Also known as pepitas, these are the hulled seeds of a pumpkin. They are rich in iron, magnesium, and protein (a 30g serving has more protein than an egg) and an excellent source of fiber and the heart-healthy amino acid tryptophan. Add to granola, bread, and cookies or roast with a few pinches of sea salt, tamari, and chile flakes for a delicious snack.

Sunflower
Another winner in the plant-based protein camp, sunflower seeds are a rich source of magnesium, copper, dietary fiber, vitamins B and E and linoleic acid. They are delicious by the handful as a snack, or as a topping for salads, smoothie bowls, soups, and dips. You can also blend them to make your own creamy sunflower-seed butter.

Chia
Despite their tiny size, these ancient seeds pack a serious nutritional punch. High in fiber and omega-3s, they make a great addition to an energizing breakfast or smoothie. Although expensive, they triple in size when soaked, so you need only a small amount. They can be purchased whole or ground in most supermarkets.

Hemp
Shelled hemp seeds, also known as hemp hearts, have a smooth, nutty flavor and will fill your system with essential fatty acids, specifically heart-healthy omega-3s and omega-6s. An excellent source of protein, magnesium, and fiber, they have also been shown to reduce inflammation and balance hormones. Hemp oil is especially beneficial raw in dressings, sauces, or smoothies as a healthy supplement. It is available from health food shops and online.

Flaxseeds/Linseeds
These little seeds are high in fiber and one of the best dietary sources of omega-3 essential fatty acids, having both anti-inflammatory and antioxidant properties and also promoting cardiovascular and colon health. Although I do enjoy the texture of these seeds whole, they are best absorbed when eaten ground or milled. You can find milled flaxseed in supermarkets or you can grind them yourself. Flax is a brilliant source of compounds known as lignans, which have been shown to protect against cancer.

STORING NUTS & SEEDS

A handful of raw nuts and seeds is a good choice when you're in need of a healthy snack. They're easy to travel with and also keep well at home if you follow these tips.

◆ **Put a lid on it** Transfer your nuts and seeds to airtight containers. This keeps air out, which makes for fresher nuts and seeds, and protects them from other odors, which are easily absorbed by nuts and seeds because of their high oil content.

◆ **Keep them cool** They last at room temperature for a few months. To keep them fresh for longer, store them in the fridge or freezer: in general, they'll stay fresh for up to 6 months in the refrigerator and for up to one year in the freezer.

NUTS & SEEDS TO SAVOR

When it comes to eating I believe in balance, and a little bit of what you fancy does you good. Combining everyday, kitchen staples with fresh, seasonal ingredients, you will discover how easy it is to make tempting, nourishing, and well-balanced meals.

I've drawn inspiration from regions far and wide, with a selection of colorful dishes that taps into the vibrancy and flair of Middle-Eastern and Mediterranean cuisine. Nuts and seeds especially appreciate spice, sweetness, sour, and saltiness, so you'll find an array of creative variations and generous depth of flavor to suit all tastes. These dishes are nutrient-dense and delicious, leaving you feeling happier, healthier, and more energized.

MAKING YOUR OWN

These key recipes are easily tweaked—whether you add spice to your nut butter or natural sweetness to your milk, the possibilities are endless. Despite the myriad of store-bought varieties now, I love the versatility that comes with making your own nut milks, butters, or flours at home.

Makes about 4 cups

5 ounces nuts or seeds of your choice
Pinch of sea salt
1 teaspoon spices of your choice (see right)
2 to 4 Medjool dates (optional, or 1 tablespoon agave, date, or maple syrup)

NUT MILK

Spices add extra flavor: try cinnamon, vanilla bean paste or extract, cardamom seeds, mixed spice, or turmeric. Or add coffee, cacao, or cocoa powder.

1. Place the nuts or seeds in a large bowl, cover with water, and leave to soak for 4 to 6 hours, or preferably overnight. (Soaking aids the body's ability to absorb nutrients, making the nuts more beneficial, nutritious, and easily digested; almonds and hazelnuts need a couple of hours more (see tip); hemp seeds do not require soaking).
2. Drain the nuts or seeds, rinse under cold water and put into a high-speed blender or food-processor. Add the remaining ingredients with 4 cups of cold water and process until smooth.
3. Taste and adjust the sweetness and spices to your liking, adding more if necessary.
4. Strain the milk through a fine cloth or fine mesh sieve into a large bowl. Discard the solids. Stored in the fridge in a covered pitcher or glass bottle it will keep for 3 to 4 days.

Sprouting Nuts and Seeds

By completing several cycles of soaking, rinsing, draining, and air exposure over a period of a few days, some seeds enter a state of germination in which sprouts appear. Sprouting occurs far more readily in seeds (e.g. pumpkin, sunflower, and sesame seeds). This extent of germination is highly beneficial; promoting enzyme activity further than soaking and multiplying nutrients, vitamins, and amino acids into more easily digestible forms.

NUT BUTTER

Makes 10 ounces

10 ounces nuts or seeds of
  your choice (or a mixture)
Pinch of salt
1 teaspoon honey or other
  natural sweetener such as
  agave, date, or maple syrup
  (optional)
½ teaspoon spices of your
  choice, e.g. cinnamon,
  mixed spice, ground
  ginger, vanilla (optional)

One of the best things to spread on your bread or add
to a smoothie first thing in the morning, nut or seed
butter is indulgent and fantastically good for you. Choose
good-quality, very fresh raw almonds, hazelnuts, cashews,
or walnuts. Roasting the nuts first will give the butter a
richer taste and creamier texture.

1. Process the nuts or seeds with a pinch of salt in a food-
processor or high-speed blender until you obtain a creamy
paste. As the nuts are blending, add either a little honey (or
other natural sweetener) or water to help the mixture form
into an emulsified butter, then add the spices (if using).
2. Store in an airtight container or lidded jar in the fridge. It
will keep for up to 3 months.

NUT FLOUR

Makes 1 pound

1 pound nuts or seeds of
  your choice (or a mixture)

Nut flours come in all sorts of varieties and make a
super low-carb and grain-free alternative to standard
grain flours. Technically, if the skin is still on the nut, it
is considered "meal" rather than flour, but I recommend
using blanched nuts. There is nothing to stop you
from experimenting with seeds too. Nut flours take
very little time to make and can be substantially
cheaper than shop-bought alternatives.

Place the nuts or seeds in a high-speed blender or
food-processor and pulse until they are as finely ground
as you like, scraping the sides of the bowl with a flat-
bladed knife from time to time. This shouldn't take more
than about 10 to 20 seconds: if you process
them for much longer they will
turn into butter. To help avoid this,
make sure that the processor bowl
and blade are dry and cool and the
nuts are at room temperature.

In general,
brown-skinned nuts
and seeds contain
higher levels of
enzyme inhibitors
and need to be soaked
for several hours
to ensure complete
digestion.

GROUND

ORANGE, POPPY & PISTACHIO MUFFINS

*VEGETARIAN *GLUTEN-FREE *DAIRY-FREE

These versatile muffins, made with a combination of almond and coconut flour, are lovely and light. They're perfect for breakfast-on-the-run, a healthy snack at work or an afternoon pick-me-up with a lovely brew. Make a batch on the weekend and you'll be set for the week ahead.

Makes 8

⅔ cup pistachios, plus 1½ tablespoons chopped
1 cup almond flour (see page 13) or ground almonds
½ cup coconut flour
¼ cup brown or coconut sugar
1 teaspoon baking powder
Pinch of sea salt
Zest and juice of 1 large orange
1 tablespoon poppy seeds, plus 1 teaspoon
Approx. ¼ cup almond milk (see page 12)
4 large eggs, lightly beaten
3 tablespoons almond oil
1 teaspoon vanilla bean paste or extract

1. Preheat the oven to 350°F. Line 8 cups of a 12-cup muffin pan with paper baking cups.

2. Place ⅔ cup pistachios in a food-processor or a high-speed blender and process until very fine. Place the nuts into a large bowl and stir in the almond flour, coconut flour, sugar, baking powder, salt, orange zest, and poppy seeds.

3. Squeeze the juice of the orange into a measuring cup, then add the almond milk to make ¾ cup. Pour over the dry ingredients and add the beaten eggs, almond oil, and vanilla bean paste or extract (or put all the ingredients into an electric mixer). Process or stir until smooth and combined.

4. Spoon the mixture into the cups and top each one with the remaining poppy seeds and chopped pistachios. Bake for 25 to 30 minutes or until golden, cooked through, and firm to the touch.

5. Leave the muffins to cool slightly in the pan for 5 minutes before transferring out onto a wire rack to cool completely.

WAFFLES & DATE CHOCOLATE SAUCE

*VEGETARIAN *GLUTEN-FREE *DAIRY-FREE

Decadent yet wholesome, these are drizzled with warm, sticky sauce and vibrant fresh berries for an indulgent affair to savor. Golden and crispy on the outside with a soft and fluffy center, these healthy treats contain gluten-free buckwheat flour, supplying a multitude of vitamins and minerals. These provide a little sweet solace on wet and windy days and are sure to warm the hearts of family and friends.

Makes 3 to 4 (depending on the size of your waffle iron)

½ cup buckwheat flour
⅔ cup almond flour (see page 13) or ground almonds
2 teaspoons baking powder
½ teaspoon salt
2 tablespoons date syrup (or unrefined sugar)
1 egg, lightly beaten
1 cup plus 2 tablespoons almond milk (see page 12)
2 tablespoons almond butter (see page 12)
2 teaspoons vanilla bean paste or extract

For the date chocolate sauce
6 tablespoons date syrup
6 tablespoons raw cacao powder
2½ tablespoons maple syrup

To serve
1¾ cups fresh red berries, such as raspberries or strawberries
¼ cup toasted slivered almonds

1. Sift both flours, the baking powder, and salt into a mixing bowl and stir to combine. Add the date syrup, egg, almond milk, almond butter, and vanilla bean paste or extract, then mix well until combined. Leave the batter to rest for 5 minutes.

2. Make the date and chocolate sauce by heating all the ingredients together in a small pan over a gentle heat. Stir until combined and glossy, then set aside until needed.

3. Preheat a waffle iron as per instructions, spray both sides of the iron with oil spray (I use coconut oil) and pour a large ladleful (about ⅔ cup) of batter in the center of the iron and spread out towards the edges with an offset spatula. Close the lid and allow to cook. Repeat until all the batter is used.

4. Serve the waffles with the fresh fruit, a drizzle of date chocolate sauce and the toasted almonds.

HAZELNUT, LETTUCE & PEA SOUP

*VEGETARIAN *GLUTEN-FREE

If you're looking for something low in fat, high in protein and yet big on flavor, this vibrant green soup checks all the right boxes—perfect as a dinner party starter or just for those times when you crave a bowl of steaming comfort. You may not have used nuts in a soup before, but they really work, adding great texture and richness. Can be made ahead and stored in the fridge for up to a week.

Serves 4 to 6

2 tablespoons butter
2 spring onions, thinly sliced
1 large garlic clove, roughly
  chopped
1 large round lettuce or
  2 small (approx. 14 ounces),
  washed and roughly chopped
1 pound frozen garden peas
1½ cups hazelnuts, finely
  ground
4 cups vegetable (or chicken)
  stock
A handful of fresh mint leaves
Salt and pepper

To serve
¼ cup toasted hazelnuts,
  chopped
A few fresh mint leaves
1 spring onion, thinly sliced
4 to 6 tablespoons plain
  yogurt or crème fraîche

1. Melt the butter in a large pan on a medium heat. Add the spring onion and garlic, then gently cook until softened (but not browned).

2. Add the lettuce leaves and allow to wilt for a few minutes, then add the peas, ground hazelnuts, stock, and mint leaves. Bring to the boil, then reduce the heat to a gentle simmer for a further 5 to 6 minutes. Season with salt and pepper.

3. Remove the pan from the heat and pour into a high-speed blender. Blitz the soup until smooth and creamy, then check the seasoning.

4. Pour the soup into bowls and scatter over the hazelnuts, mint leaves, and spring onion and add a spoonful of yogurt or crème fraîche.

For a non-vegetarian option, top with slices of crispy pan-fried pancetta before serving.

GOAT CHEESE & BEET TART

*VEGETARIAN

This vegetarian tart combines the perfect marriage of goat cheese, beet, fresh thyme, and toasted pine nuts—ideal for a midweek meal, a weekend lunch with friends or enjoyed cold with a crisp green salad on a picnic. And as a bonus, the irresistible pine-nut crust is a simple way to add extra nutty crunch—and requires no kneading.

Serves 6 to 8

For the base

1⅛ cup pine nuts, finely ground
1 cup buckwheat or almond flour (see page 13)
½ cup rolled oats
½ teaspoon sea salt
1 egg yolk
3 tablespoons butter, melted
1 tablespoon honey

1 tablespoon hemp seed oil
1 garlic clove, finely chopped
½ red onion, sliced
A handful of young spinach leaves
¼ cup garden peas, cooked
1 small raw or cooked beet, thinly sliced
2 tablespoons toasted pine nuts
2 large eggs plus 2 large yolks
⅔ cup heavy cream
⅓ cup crème fraîche
3 tablespoons goat cheese
A handful of fresh thyme leaves, plus extra to serve
1 teaspoon honey
Salt and pepper

1. Mix together all the ingredients for the base in a bowl. Line a 9-inch-diameter, 1-inch-deep loose-bottomed tart pan. Starting from the center, press the mixture evenly into the base and sides of the pan. Use a fork to prick the base to allow steam to escape, then chill for 30 minutes. Meanwhile, preheat the oven to 350°F and place a metal baking sheet inside the oven to heat up.

2. Place the tart pan on of the baking sheet and bake for 10 minutes, or until lightly golden and firm to the touch. Set aside to cool.

3. For the filling, heat the oil in a large pan and gently cook the garlic with the onion until soft but not colored. Spoon into the crust, then add the spinach leaves, peas, and beet with 1 tablespoon of the pine nuts. Mix the eggs, cream, and crème fraîche together in a measuring cup. Slowly pour the mixture on top of the vegetables, then evenly divide the goat cheese on top and scatter over the thyme. Season with salt and pepper. Return the tart to the baking sheet and cook for 35 minutes, or until the filling is just set in the middle.

4. Leave to cool for 15 minutes, then remove the sides of the pan. Before serving, top the tart with the extra thyme leaves and pine nuts, and drizzle over the honey.

Pine nuts are an excellent source of plant-derived nutrients, essential minerals, vitamins, and "heart friendly" mono-unsaturated fats.

ONE-PAN ROASTED PESTO CHICKEN *GLUTEN-FREE

This one-pan wonder dish, which brings together some of my favorite flavors, can be prepared in a flash. The peppery and nutty pesto adds pep, while the aniseed of the fennel, together with the toasty pine nuts and zesty lemon, meld into something new and delicious. Serve with crusty bread to mop up all the lovely pan juices and/or boiled new potatoes.

Serves 4

For the pesto
About 1 cup watercress, plus extra to serve
A large handful of basil leaves
1 garlic clove
Zest of 1 small lemon, plus 1 tablespoon juice
¼ cup pine nuts
1 tablespoon walnuts
1 ounce Pecorino, grated (about ¼ cup)
⅓ cup good-quality canola, olive, or walnut oil
Salt and pepper

2 tablespoons olive or canola oil
4 chicken legs
2 fennel bulbs, sliced
2 garlic heads, sliced in half horizontally
1 large lemon, cut into small wedges (or use any leftover lemon from pesto)
Leaves from a few fresh thyme sprigs
1 tablespoon pine nuts

1. Preheat the oven to 400°F. Begin by making the pesto. Place all the ingredients except the oil and seasoning into a food-processor. Start the motor running and slowly add the oil, blending until the pesto comes together but is still a bit chunky and not too smooth. (This should take only 2 minutes.) Season to taste.

2. Heat 1 tablespoon of the oil in a large pan and brown the chicken legs all over. Arrange the chicken, fennel, garlic, lemon wedges, and thyme (reserving a few leaves for garnish) in a roasting pan and spread into one layer. Drizzle over the remaining oil and season with salt and pepper. Roast in the oven for 35 minutes.

3. Remove the pan from the oven, then spoon over some of the pesto and scatter over the pine nuts. Return to the oven for a further 10 minutes, or until the chicken is golden and cooked through.

4. Serve with any leftover pesto, some fresh watercress, and thyme leaves.

Canola and walnut oil, as well as other nut and seed oils, will keep well in the refrigerator for up to 2 years

ZA'ATAR CRUNCHY CHICKEN & TAHINI *DAIRY-FREE

This crunchy baked chicken coating is so delicious and healthy, offering a high-fiber gluten-free alternative to breadcrumbs. I adore the savory crisp coating against the creamy sweet-and-spicy dipping sauce—a match made in heaven!

Serves 4

6 skinless and boneless chicken thighs, trimmed of fat (or 4 skinless breasts)
2 tablespoons honey
1 tablespoon tahini
4 tablespoons za'atar
½ cup blanched almonds, roughly ground
½ cup rolled quinoa flakes (or rolled oats)
1½ tablespoons white and/or black sesame seeds
Salt and pepper
A handful of cilantro, roughly chopped, to serve

For the miso sesame dip
2½ tablespoons sweet white miso
2 tablespoons sesame oil
Juice of 1 lime
1½ tablespoons tahini
1 to 2 red chiles, finely chopped
1 spring onion, finely sliced

1. Preheat the oven to 400°F and line a large baking sheet with parchment paper.

2. Slice the chicken thighs lengthways into two or three strips (or the breasts into four or five), depending on their size. Place the honey and tahini in a shallow dish or bowl. Add the chicken and toss to coat. Transfer to the fridge, covered, to marinate for 1 hour.

3. In a bowl, mix together the za'atar, almonds, quinoa flakes, and sesame seeds with a good pinch of salt and pepper. Remove the chicken from the fridge and, taking one chicken strip at a time, shake off the excess marinade, then toss in the za'atar mixture until evenly coated. Transfer to the prepared baking trays and bake for 20 to 25 minutes, or until golden, crispy, and cooked through.

4. Meanwhile, make the dipping sauce by whisking together the miso, sesame oil, lime juice, and tahini with 1 tablespoon of water until smooth. Stir in the chile and spring onion, then season to taste. Serve the hot chicken strips sprinkled with some cilantro, with the dipping sauce alongside.

Za'atar, which is available in the spice section of most large supermarkets, boosts the flavor of a marinade or can be sprinkled over Greek yogurt and drizzled with sesame seed oil for a dip that's perfect with pita!

ALMOND & SPELT FLOUR SODA BREAD

*VEGETARIAN

The scent of freshly baked bread as you cut into your own homemade loaf is heavenly. The combination of spelt, almond, and the variety of seeds packs each slice with a nutritional punch high in vitamin B2, niacin, thiamin, and magnesium. The soft crumb texture of this bread makes it the ideal partner for my Cashew, Olive & Seed Tapenade (see page 54) and it is delicious toasted, then spread with nut or seed butter.

Makes 2 small loaves, each serving 6, or 1 large loaf to serve 12

1½ cups almond flour (see page 13) or ground almonds
1½ cups spelt flour
2 teaspoons baking soda
1 teaspoon salt
⅔ cup mixed seeds, e.g. chia, sunflower, pumpkin, linseed, poppy, sesame (look for bags of mixed seeds in supermarkets)
¾ cup plus 2 tablespoons buttermilk
⅓ cup plus 2 tablespoons almond milk (see page 12)
1 teaspoon date nectar or honey
Oil, for greasing
1 tablespoon almond milk

1. Preheat the oven to 425°F. Sift the flours, baking soda, and salt into a large bowl and stir in the seeds, leaving 2 tablespoons for the topping. Make a well in the center and add the buttermilk, almond milk, and honey. Stir to combine: the dough should be slightly sticky.

2. Turn the mixture out onto a work surface lightly floured with one or both flours and briefly knead until you have a smooth dough. Divide in half, then, using your hands, shape into two oval or round loaves (or leave as one loaf if you wish). Transfer to a lightly oiled, then floured non-stick baking sheet. Use a sharp knife to cut a deep cross in the top, then brush with a little almond milk and sprinkle over the remaining seeds.

3. Bake for 40 minutes, or until the bread is golden and sounds hollow when the bottom is tapped. If you're making one large loaf you'll need to leave it in the oven for a further 5 minutes. (If the seeds begin to brown too much, cover with a sheet of foil at this stage.)

4. Leave to cool for a few minutes, then transfer onto a wire rack. This bread stays moist for 3 to 4 days. Alternatively, you can freeze it until needed.

NECTARINES WITH MACADAMIA CRUMB

*VEGETARIAN

I am particularly enamored with this recipe: the soft flesh of the poached nectarines are given a warming kick from the ginger wine and they take on a whole new dimension when paired with the crunchy macadamia and gingersnap crumb. As an alternative to ginger wine, you could use Madeira (or other sweet wine) or ginger cordial.

Serves 6

For the poached nectarines
6 nectarines
1¼ cups ginger wine
5 tablespoons honey
1 tablespoon vanilla bean paste or 1 vanilla pod, seeds removed (pod reserved)

For the macadamia crumb
3 gingersnap cookies (or any ginger cookie variety)
⅓ cup macadamia nuts

Yogurt or crème fraîche, to serve

1. Cut a small cross in the base of each nectarine, put in a large bowl and cover with boiling water. Leave for 1 minute, then drain and, when cool enough to handle, peel off the skin and discard.

2. Put the wine, honey, and vanilla paste or seeds, in a saucepan large enough to fit the nectarines snugly. Add ¾ cup just-boiled water from the kettle, place the pan over a medium–low heat and bring to a gentle simmer, stirring until the honey dissolves. Add the nectarines to the pan (and the reserved vanilla pod, if using) and pour in a little more water if needed to just cover the fruit. Loosely place a lid on top to allow steam to escape and poach for 5 minutes, or until the nectarines have slightly softened.

3. Briefly blitz the cookies and macadamias together in a food-processor or high-speed blender.

4. Serve each nectarine with spoonfuls of the syrup, some macadamia crumb, and yogurt or crème fraîche on the side.

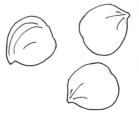

GRILLED PINEAPPLE & COCONUT WHIP

*VEGETARIAN *GLUTEN-FREE *DAIRY-FREE

I love caramelising fragrant fruits this way. They're delicious served as I have suggested here, as a hearty brunch with granola, toasted oats, or quinoa, or even as a pudding with crushed meringue. Treat this recipe as a rough guide and feel free to experiment—most firm fruit grills well.

Serves 6 to 8

For the pineapple
1 medium pineapple, sliced into rings (larger ones halved)
⅓ cup honey
Zest of 1 lime, plus a squeeze of juice

For the coconut whip
13.5-ounce can coconut milk, refrigerated for 2 to 3 hours (or preferably overnight)
1 teaspoon vanilla bean paste or extract

To serve
A handful of Greek basil leaves (or ordinary basil, larger leaves torn)
2 tablespoons mix of milled flax, chia seed, apple & cinnamon (I like Linwoods; see right)

1. Preheat the oven to 350°F. Spread the pineapple slices out on a baking tray, then drizzle with honey and the lime zest and juice to evenly cover. Roast for 25 minutes, or until golden and sticky.

2. Remove the coconut milk from the fridge, then carefully remove the solids—usually just over half a can/about 1 cup (reserve the remaining milk for another use)—and place into the bowl of an electric mixer (or a bowl). Whip the coconut on a medium speed until soft peaks form. Stir in the vanilla paste or extract until combined.

3. Serve the pineapple slices with the remaining honey syrup from the baking tray, spoonfuls of coconut whip and scattered with the basil leaves and the flax, chia seed, apple, and cinnamon mix.

If you can't find a flax, chia seed, apple, and cinnamon mix, finely grind 1 tablespoon of chia seeds in a high-speed blender or spice grinder and stir together with 1 tablespoon of milled flaxseeds and a pinch of cinnamon.

APPLE, NUT & SEED CRACKERS

*VEGETARIAN *GLUTEN-FREE *DAIRY-FREE

Not only are seeds a wonderful source of healthy fats, but they also offer a good dose of vitamin E, which acts as an antioxidant to protect cells from the damage caused by free radicals. Here, the seeds add extra crunch to the crackers as well as a good dose of protein.

Makes 25 to 30

½ cup pumpkin seeds
½ cup sunflower seeds
¼ cup each brown linseeds or flaxseeds, hemp seeds, chia seeds, and black or white sesame seeds
⅔ cup almond or amaranth flour (see page 13)
1½ teaspoons salt
⅓ cup plus 2 tablespoons apple juice, plus 2 tablespoons for topping
¼ cup almond or olive oil
2 tablespoons sunflower seed butter (see page 13)
⅔ cup almond milk (see page 12)
1 tablespoon honey (or maple syrup, if vegan)

1. Preheat the oven to 300°F. Line two half sheet baking pans (13 × 18 inches) with parchment paper.

2. Stir all the seeds together in a bowl, then remove about a third for the topping and set aside. Add the remaining ingredients, except the 2 tablespoons of apple juice and the honey, along with ¼ cup water, and stir together until you have a loose but not runny batter (add more water or almond milk if needed).

3. Pour the batter onto the baking pans and, using a knife or offset spatula, smooth out thinly. Bake for 25 minutes.

4. Whisk together the 2 tablespoons apple juice and honey in a small bowl then brush the glaze over the crackers and sprinkle over the remaining seeds. Slice into roughly 2½-inch squares and bake for a further 30 minutes, or until the crackers are hard and crunchy. Remove to a wire rack to cool.

These crunchy crackers pair perfectly with a soft blue cheese, such as Roquefort or Gorgonzola dolce, and some fig chutney.

FRUITY ALMOND & SEED CRUMBLE

*VEGETARIAN

This recipe encapsulates all that is right about a hot, sweet, and incredibly comforting dessert that has the power to elicit "need-it-now" cravings! Chunks of apple and strawberry add just the right amount of natural sweetness to contrast with the tart rhubarb, and the almond, hazelnut, and pecan crumble gives it its signature flavor and texture. A perfect marriage of fruit, nuts, and seeds.

Serves 8

For the filling

3 medium apples
14 ounces rhubarb
1 quart strawberries
Zest and juice of 1 orange
1 tablespoon vanilla bean paste or extract
¼ cup maple syrup

For the crumble

½ cup plus 2 tablespoons butter, chilled and diced
1⅓ cup almond flour (see page 13)
⅔ cup all-purpose flour
½ teaspoon each ground cinnamon and pie spice
Pinch of salt
¼ cup unrefined demerara sugar (or maple syrup)
½ cup rolled oats
¼ cup each blanched almonds, blanched hazelnuts, and pecans, roughly chopped (or any nuts of your choice)
1 tablespoon sunflower seeds
½ tablespoon linseeds

1. Preheat the oven to 400°F.

2. Prepare the filling ingredients: peel, core, and chop the apples into bite-size chunks, slice the rhubarb into small pieces and slice the strawberries in half (or quarters, if large). Place all the filling ingredients into a shallow 2-litre ovenproof dish and stir together.

3. For the crumble, put the butter, flours, spices, and a pinch of salt into a large bowl and rub together with your fingers until the mixture resembles coarse breadcrumbs. (Alternatively, use a food-processor.) Add the sugar and oats and stir to combine. Sprinkle the crumble mix evenly over the fruit, then top with the chopped nuts and the seeds.

4. Bake for 40 minutes, or until golden and bubbling. Check the crumble after 30 minutes and cover with foil if the nuts are beginning to brown, to prevent them burning.

5. Serve with custard, ice cream, or yogurt mixed with some vanilla bean paste, if you wish.

One of the healthiest, most protein-rich foods in their raw, unsalted form, almonds also contain high levels of healthy, monounsaturated fats.

PEACH MELBA CHEESECAKE

*VEGETARIAN *GLUTEN-FREE *DAIRY-FREE

This make-ahead frozen raw cheesecake is my interpretation of the much-celebrated dessert Peach Melba, combining peaches and raspberries with a delicious nutty crust base. This healthy take on the traditional cheesecake is the ultimate showstopper.

Serves 10 to 12

For the nut crust base

1 cup each pecans, cashews, and shredded unsweetened coconut

½ cup soft Medjool dates, pits removed

¼ teaspoon salt

Zest of 1 lime

2 tablespoons milled flaxseed (optional)

For the peach layer

4 cups cashews, soaked for 2 to 3 hours (or preferably overnight)

5 fresh peaches, pits removed (or 2 × 14-ounce cans sliced peaches, drained)

1 frozen banana

⅓ cup plus 2 tablespoons coconut cream

½ cup maple syrup

1 teaspoon vanilla bean paste or extract

1 tablespoon tahini

For the raspberry layer

1 cup frozen raspberries

1 to 2 tablespoons maple

1. Grease and line a 8-inch springform cake pan. Grind the pecans, cashews, coconut, and dates in a food-processor or high-speed blender. Stir in the salt, lime zest, and flaxseed (if using) to form a sticky dough and press firmly into the bottom of the pan. Place in the freezer for 30 minutes, until hardened.

2. For the peach layer, drain and rinse the cashews. Place all the ingredients into a food-processor or high-speed blender and process until smooth. Pour about two thirds of the mixture over the top of the base. Place in the freezer for about 45 minutes, or until the layer is firm.

3. Meanwhile, make the raspberry layer by adding the raspberries and maple syrup to the remaining peach mixture and blend again. Spoon the raspberry layer on top of the frozen peach layer and leave to freeze for 2 to 3 hours, or preferably overnight.

4. Remove the cheesecake from the freezer about 30 minutes before serving and decorate with frozen peach slices, raspberries, shredded coconut, and some chia/hemp seeds, if you wish.

Cashews are packed full of magnesium, which lowers blood pressure and works alongside copper to increase bone strength. Contrary to belief, they mainly contain good, healthy fats and zero cholesterol.

CHIA, RASPBERRY & COCONUT BARS

*GLUTEN-FREE *DAIRY-FREE

Imagine a childhood treat that has graduated and gone to college—these delicious bars are both gratifying and nutritious. With the inclusion of super seeds hemp and chia, they are rich in omega-3s, packed with protein, antioxidants, and fiber, and naturally gluten- and dairy-free to boot.

Serves 10 to 12

For the base
1 ¾ cups almond flour (see page 13) or ground almonds
1½ cups shredded unsweetened coconut
¼ cup date syrup
1 egg, lightly beaten
2 tablespoons hemp seeds
¼ teaspoon sea salt
⅓ cup almond or coconut oil, melted

For the raspberry layer
1¼ cups raspberry jam
1 tablespoon white chia seeds

For the coconut cream
¼-ounce package powdered unflavored gelatin
1¼ cups coconut cream
¾ cup plus 2 tablespoons almond milk (see page 12)
2 tablespoons maple syrup
1 tablespoon vanilla bean paste or extract

For the topping
⅔ cup almond or coconut oil, melted
1⅓ cups cacao powder, plus 1 tablespoon to dust

1. Preheat the oven to 350°F. Grease and line a 8.5 × 4.5 × 2.5-inch straight-sided loaf pan with parchment paper (cut a piece larger than the pan so you can use the overhanging edges as handles to remove the loaf later).

2. To make the base, mix together all the ingredients, then press evenly into the bottom of the pan. Bake for 20 minutes, or until lightly golden. Remove from the oven and set aside to cool.

3. Stir together the jam and chia seeds in a bowl, then set aside. Stir the gelatin in a bowl with 2 tablespoons cold water and let sit for 5 minutes to absorb. Meanwhile, heat the coconut cream and almond milk in a pan over a medium heat.

4. Add the gelatin to the coconut cream mixture in the pan, stirring until dissolved. Strain into a bowl and set aside to cool. Stir in the maple syrup and vanilla.

5. Spoon the jam in a layer on top of the base, then place the pan in the fridge for 30 to 45 minutes, or until the jam is soft set. Carefully pour the coconut cream mixture on top of the layer of jam. Return to the fridge to chill for 2 to 3 hours, or until firm and set.

6. Combine the oil with the cacao powder and stir until smooth. Gently remove the loaf from the parchment paper and transfer to a wire rack set over a tray. Pour the topping mixture over the top, then, working quickly, tilt the rack from side to side slightly to allow the topping to evenly coat the edges. Leave to set at room temperature for 15 to 20 minutes, then dust with extra cacao and cut into slices.

KEY LIME
MATCHA PIE

I love a twist on a classic and this key lime matcha pie is as delicious as it is healthy. Enjoyable at any time of day and perfect for an after-dinner, guilt-free dessert. The addictive nut, fig, and coconut crust provides the perfect base for the creamy filling. Zesty, clean-feeling desserts like this are the kind of food pleasure we should all be indulging in.

Serves 10 to 12

For the crust
1 cup pistachios
⅓ cup walnuts
6 soft, sticky dried figs
1½ cups shredded
   unsweetened coconut
A good squeeze of lime juice

For the filling
1¾ cups cashews, soaked for
   2 to 3 hours (or preferably
   overnight)
Zest and juice of 3 limes,
   plus extra zest to decorate
¾ cup plus 2 tablespoons
   coconut cream
⅓ cup plus 2 tablespoons
   maple syrup
1¾ teaspoons matcha powder

Matcha, a Japanese green-tea powder, contains a multitude of health benefits, including powerful antioxidants, vitamin C and fiber. It has a delicious, distinct flavor and can be found in health food shops, Asian supermarkets, and online.

1. Pulse the pistachios and walnuts in a food-processor or high-speed blender until finely ground. Add the figs, coconut, and lime juice and pulse until combined. The mixture should easily form into a ball. If it's not sticky enough, add more figs and lime juice until you reach the desired consistency.

2. Press the mixture into the base and sides of a lined 9-inch loose-bottomed tart pan. Place in the fridge to chill until needed.

3. For the filling, drain the cashews, rinse, and put in a high-speed blender with 3 tablespoons of water. Process until a paste is formed. Add the lime zest and juice, coconut cream, and maple syrup and blend together on high until smooth. Remove ⅔ cup of the lime cream and set aside, then add 1½ teaspoons of the matcha powder to the main mix and blend again.

4. Remove the crust from the fridge and fill with the matcha lime cream. Spread with the back of a spoon so that it covers the crust evenly. Pour the remaining lime cream into the blender and add ¼ teaspoon of matcha powder, and whizz until blended. Spoon into the center of the tart on top of the darker lime cream, then use a skewer or cocktail stick to create swirl patterns with the two layers. Return the tart to the fridge to set for at least 2 hours, or preferably overnight.

5. Just before serving, decorate with lime zest, if you wish.

MILK, OIL, & BUTTER

ALMOND & CHERRY GRANOLA ICE POPS

*VEGETARIAN

Fuss-free wholesome yogurt ice pops that count as one of your five-a-day, topped with crunchy granola for a delicious and refreshing frozen treat. With their pretty pop of color and irresistible fruity burst, the sweet and juicy cherries contain antioxidant anthocyanins. Essential healthy feasting on a balmy day.

*Makes 10 ice pops
(You will need a mold
for 10 ice pops)*

1¼ cups Greek yogurt
¾ cup almond milk
   (see page 12)
2 tablespoons maple syrup
1 teaspoon vanilla bean
   paste or extract
½ cup granola (store-bought
   or see page 67)
1 cup cherries, pitted and
   halved

1. Stir together the yogurt, almond milk, maple syrup, and vanilla until combined.

2. To assemble, divide the granola among the ice pop molds, then top with the almond mixture and finally with the cherries. (The layers don't need to be perfect—it makes for prettier ice pops if they're not!)

3. Cover the top of the mold and freeze until firm, about 4 hours.

4. To remove the ice pops, run the mold under hot water for 10 seconds before releasing each one gently. Store in the freezer until ready to eat. Drizzle with more maple syrup to serve, if you wish.

If you don't have
ice pop molds, freeze the
whole mixture of yogurt in
a freeze-proof container,
stir in the cherries, and
scatter the granola over the
surface, then simply scoop
out servings as you wish.

HAZELNUT MILK PLUM OATMEAL

*VEGETARIAN *DAIRY-FREE

Crunchy toasted hazelnuts pair perfectly with creamy hazelnut milk oatmeal and roasted sweet plum compote in this rewarding breakfast dish. If you have time to toast the oats before hunger takes over, it is well worth the effort. This could easily become a tempting weekend staple.

Serves 2

1 cup rolled oats
1⅔ cup hazelnut milk
   (see page 12)
1 teaspoon vanilla bean
   paste or extract
½ teaspoon ground cinnamon
A grating of fresh nutmeg
¼ teaspoon sea salt

For the plum compote
3 plums, pits removed, sliced
   into segments
2 tablespoons maple syrup,
   honey, or agave nectar
Zest of ½ lemon

To serve
¼ cup toasted hazelnuts,
   chopped
Maple syrup, honey, or
   agave nectar

1. Make the plum compote by putting all the ingredients into a pan with 1 tablespoon of water. Over a gentle heat, cook the plums until they begin to soften, but are still holding their shape. Set aside until needed.

2. Put the oats in a pan over a medium heat and toast for 4 to 5 minutes, or until lightly browned. Transfer the oats to a saucepan and add the hazelnut milk, vanilla, spices, and salt. Bring to a simmer and cook, stirring occasionally, until soft and thickened. (Add more hazelnut milk, 1 tablespoon at a time, if you need to loosen the mixture.)

3. Serve the oatmeal in bowls with the plum compote and some of the plum juices, a drizzle of maple syrup (or honey or agave nectar) and a sprinkling of toasted chopped hazelnuts.

CASHEW & ACAI BERRY SMOOTHIE BOWL

*VEGETARIAN *GLUTEN-FREE *DAIRY-FREE

Smoothies are a super, simple fast track to flavor and nourishment. The wonder berry acai has delicious fruity, almost red-wine notes with chocolate overtones and is packed full of micronutrients and almost double the antioxidants of blueberries. I love to top my smoothie bowls with swirls of silky pumpkin seed butter, but you could try any other variety of nut or seed butter you like (see page 13).

Serves 2

1 cup raw cashews (soaked
   for 2 to 3 hours, or
   preferably overnight,
   if time)
1 large banana, peeled,
   chopped, and frozen
¼ cup each raspberries,
   blackberries, and
   strawberries
⅓ cup cashew milk
   (see page 12)
1 tablespoon acai berry
   powder
1 tablespoon linseeds

For the topping
1 tablespoon pumpkin seed
   butter (see page 13)
A handful of mixed fresh
   berries
Seeds, such as chia,
   pumpkin, and sunflower
A few edible flowers
   (optional)

1. Drain and rinse the cashews, then place into a blender with all the ingredients for the smoothie and blitz until smooth.

2. Allow the mixture to stand and thicken for 1 minute then blend for a further 10 seconds.

3. Divide the mixture into bowls and serve with a swirl of pumpkin seed butter and topped with fresh berries, a mixture of your favorite seeds and a few edible flowers, if you wish.

GREEN CASHEW SMOOTHIE
*VEGETARIAN *GLUTEN-FREE *DAIRY-FREE

"Eat your greens" I was always told. Now, thanks to this smoothie recipe, you can with ease! This is a super-stealthy way to reap all the goodness—it's packed with cashews, apple, spinach, cucumber, and avocado, with the added virtues of hemp and chia seeds. "Power" powders are optional here and can be found in most larger supermarkets, health food shops, and online. When a smoothie tastes this good, it really is easy to go green!

Serves 4
(makes about 4 cups)

⅔ cup raw cashews, soaked for 2 to 3 hours (or preferably overnight)
2 green apples, peeled, cored, and chopped into chunks
1 kiwi fruit, peeled and chopped into chunks
1 banana, peeled, sliced, and frozen
A large handful of spinach leaves
½ ripe avocado, sliced in half
½ cucumber, seeded and sliced into large chunks
6 tablespoons cashew milk (see page 12)
1 tablespoon hemp seed powder, spirulina, or wheatgrass powder
1 teaspoon mix of hemp and chia seeds, to serve

1. Drain and rinse the cashews. Put all the ingredients except the hemp and chia seeds into a high-speed blender and blend until smooth.

2. Divide the smoothie between four glasses and serve with the hemp and chia seeds sprinkled on top.

If you wish to make this smoothie sweeter, you can add 1 tablespoon of agave or maple syrup.

SALTED CARAMEL
FRENCH TOAST
*VEGETARIAN

Perfect for those lazy weekends where you have very little desire to leave the house, this is a healthier take on traditional French toast, made with creamy hazelnut milk. The salted caramel sauce includes rich hazelnut butter making this dish a tempting sweet weekend brunch or dessert—a must for your cooking repertoire.

Serves 2

¼ cup hazelnut milk
   (see page 12)
1 egg
½ teaspoon each ground
   cinnamon and pie spice
Hazelnut (or other) oil,
   for frying
2 to 4 slices of rye, whole
   wheat, or sourdough bread

For the salted caramel sauce
6 tablespoons soft brown
   sugar
2 tablespoons butter
3 tablespoons hazelnut
   butter (see page 13)
¼ cup cream
A pinch of sea salt flakes

To serve
A handful of fresh
   strawberries, sliced
¼ cup toasted hazelnuts,
   chopped
⅓ cup hazelnut or Greek
   yogurt

1. Begin by making the salted caramel sauce. Heat all the ingredients together in a pan, stirring until the butters have melted and the sugar has dissolved. Set aside until needed.

2. In a bowl, whisk together the hazelnut milk, egg, and spices, then soak both sides of the bread until well coated and moist. Heat a little hazelnut (or other) oil in a large non-stick pan and fry the slices of bread for about 3 to 4 minutes, or until golden, on each side.

4. To serve, divide the slices of French toast between two plates and drizzle the salted caramel sauce over the top. Finish with a scattering of sliced strawberries and chopped hazelnuts and serve with the hazelnut or Greek yogurt.

If you have any left over caramel sauce (which is unlikely— it's so delicious!), it is also perfect served hot on top of ice cream.

BURRATA, BRESAOLA & NECTARINE SALAD

*GLUTEN-FREE

During the warmer months, I frequently make this for lunch. It is loosely based on the Italian classic Caprese salad—sweet, fresh, and light. Although I find grilling lends a more intense flavor and robust texture to the fruits, fresh works well too. The creaminess of burrata with the crunch of the almonds and seeds is heaven in the mouth. Simply omit the bresaola if you wish to make this vegetarian.

Serves 2

1 nectarine (or peach),
  pit removed, sliced into
  segments
½ tablespoon hemp seed oil,
  or other oil
8 to 10 slices of bresaola
7-ounce ball of burrata
  (or buffalo mozzarella)
¾ cup heirloom tomatoes
  (I like a mixture of colors),
  halved or quartered
A handful of basil leaves,
  torn if large
¼ cup toasted almonds,
  roughly chopped
1 tablespoon mixed hemp,
  sesame, sunflower, and
  pumpkin seeds
1 tablespoon hemp seed or
  pumpkin seed oil to drizzle
Salt and pepper

1. Heat a grill pan over high heat. Toss the nectarine slices in a little hemp seed oil and cook in the pan for 2 to 3 minutes on each side, or until charred. Take the pan off the heat and set aside.

2. Arrange the bresaola on a serving plate or dish. Drain the burrata from the tub and shake off any excess liquid. Tear it into pieces, then scatter it over the bresaola, followed by the tomatoes and basil leaves. Finish with a sprinkling of chopped almonds, seeds, and a good drizzle of oil. Season with some salt and pepper.

CASHEW, OLIVE & SEED TAPENADE

*VEGETARIAN *DAIRY-FREE

Bring the Mediterranean into your home with this tantalizing spread. Creamy cashews and zingy olives mixed with sunflower seeds and oregano are served on toasted seeded bread—it's the stuff of lunchtime dreams. Try this tapenade with the Almond & Spelt Flour Soda Bread on page 27, if you can eat dairy.

Makes about 1 cup

⅓ cup cashews, soaked for 2 to 3 hours (or preferably overnight)

⅓ cup sunflower seeds, soaked for 2 to 3 hours (or preferably overnight)

⅔ cup green olives with herbs and garlic

3½ tablespoons pumpkin seed or canola oil

A small handful of fresh oregano leaves, plus a few extra to serve (optional)

Salt and pepper

1. Drain and rinse the cashews and sunflower seeds and place in a food-processor or high-speed blender with all the remaining ingredients except the salt and pepper. Mix until blended but still a bit chunky. Season to taste with salt and pepper.

2. Serve on toasted seeded rye bread or similar with a few extra oregano leaves if you wish. The tapenade will keep in the fridge for up to a week in an airtight container or sealed jar.

For the ultimate feel-good smoothie bowl, boost your intake of protein and fiber while satisfying your appetite until lunchtime. I've suggested topping the smoothie with fresh raspberries, kiwi, chia, and linseeds but any favorite seasonal fruit or seed mixture would work just as well.

Serves 2 to 4
(makes about 2½ cups)

Scant 1½ cups cold almond
   milk (see page 12)
3 tablespoons black chia seeds
1 large banana, peeled, sliced,
   and frozen
1 cup frozen raspberries
2 tablespoons shredded
   unsweetened coconut
2 tablespoons linseeds
2 tablespoons honey
2 teaspoons vanilla bean
   paste or extract

To serve
Fresh mint leaves
Fresh raspberries
1 kiwi fruit, sliced
1 tablespoon mixed linseeds
   and chia seeds

1. In a measuring cup, combine ¾ cup plus 2 tablespoons of the almond milk and the chia seeds together and place in the fridge to soak for 30 minutes. Stir occasionally to remove any lumps.

2. Pour the remaining ⅔ cup of almond milk into a food-processor or high-speed blender, add the remaining ingredients and blend until smooth.

3. Stir in the thickened chia milk from the fridge then pour into glasses or bowls.

4. Serve with a few fresh mint leaves, raspberries, kiwi slices, and a sprinkling of linseeds and chia seeds.

TROPICAL CHIA LAYER DESSERT

*VEGETARIAN *GLUTEN-FREE *DAIRY-FREE

If I could bottle up the aromas of tropical heaven, then create a dessert out of it, this would be it! Some of my favorite flavor combinations—fragrant passion fruit and mango, creamy vanilla chia and toasted coconut—create a delightful contrast of textures and a feast for the senses. A simple yet impressive way to taste a little bit of paradise.

Serves 2 to 4

For the chia layer
13.5-ounce can coconut milk
4 tablespoons shredded
  unsweetened coconut
4 tablespoons white chia seeds
1 tablespoon vanilla bean
  paste or extract

For the tropical layer
1 ripe mango, peeled, stoned,
  chopped into chunks
1 tablespoon coconut almond
  butter (see right)
3 tablespoons maple syrup
1 thumb-sized piece of fresh
  ginger, peeled, and roughly
  chopped
Zest and juice of 1 lime
Seeds and pulp from
  4 passion fruit

To serve
1 to 2 passion fruit, halved
1 tablespoon coconut flakes
  (or shredded), toasted

1. Mix together the coconut milk, shredded coconut, chia seeds, and vanilla in a measuring cup or bowl and leave to thicken.

2. Put the mango flesh, coconut almond butter, maple syrup, ginger, and lime zest and juice into a high-speed blender and process until smooth, then remove and stir in the passion fruit seeds.

3. Spoon half the chia mixture into the base of two large (or four small) glasses or bowls. Cover with half the passion fruit and mango mixture. Repeat these layers.

4. Top each dessert with passion fruit and coconut before serving.

I use Pip and Nut Coconut Almond Butter, or you can use plain almond butter, if you wish.

CHOCOLATE & BRAZIL NUT BROWNIES *VEGETARIAN

Brownies are good for you, right? This less-sinful tray bake, made with spelt and an array of nuts, is packed with fiber, healthy fats, nutrients, and vitamins, as well as antioxidant-rich cacao and ginger. All of which allows you to indulge in that extra slice.

Makes 16 squares

For the ginger nut crumb
⅓ cup Brazil nuts, roughly chopped
¼ cup each walnuts and macadamia nuts, roughly chopped
1 teaspoon ground ginger
½ teaspoon pie spice
Pinch of sea salt
¼ cup crystallized ginger, finely chopped

For the brownies
1¾ cups Brazil nuts
1 stick plus 6 tablespoons unsalted butter, diced
7 ounces dark chocolate, broken into pieces
1 cup soft brown sugar
⅔ cup spelt or all-purpose flour
¼ cup raw cacao powder (or 100% cocoa powder)
¼ teaspoon baking powder
4 large eggs, lightly beaten
3 heaped tablespoons Brazil or macadamia nut butter
3.5 ounces milk chocolate, roughly chopped
2 tablespoons cacao nibs

1. Put the nuts into a food-processor and blitz until chopped but still a bit chunky. Tip into a bowl, add the remaining ginger nut crumb ingredients and stir together with 2 tablespoons of water. Set aside.

2. Preheat the oven to 350°F. Line a 9-inch baking tray with greaseproof paper.

3. Roughly chop half of the Brazil nuts and finely grind the remaining half in a food-processor.

4. In a large bowl over a pan of simmering water, melt the butter and the dark chocolate and stir until smooth. Add the chopped Brazil nuts and stir to coat. Set aside to cool to room temperature.

5. In a large bowl (or the bowl of an electric mixer), mix together the finely ground Brazil nuts, the sugar, spelt flour, cacao powder, and baking powder. Slowly add the eggs and beat until you achieve a silky consistency. Stir in the melted chocolate mixture and the Brazil nut butter, then fold in the milk chocolate chunks and cacao nibs using a spatula until evenly mixed.

6. Pour the brownie mixture into the prepared pan and smooth the surface using a spatula. Sprinkle the ginger nut crumb evenly on top then bake for 30 to 35 minutes. (Don't overcook them: the brownies should be gooey on the inside.) Cover with foil if the ginger nut crumb looks as though it is browning too much.

7. Allow to cool in the pan on a wire rack, then carefully transfer onto a board and slice into chunky squares. Dust with cacao powder if you wish. This is delicious served with a spoonful of crème fraîche or yogurt.

APRICOT, PISTACHIO & ALMOND TART

*VEGETARIAN *GLUTEN-FREE *DAIRY-FREE

Sweet, sharp, and fragrant, apricots lend themselves perfectly to this beautiful tart. The delicious sticky nut crust is packed full of nourishment and makes the perfect backdrop to the apricots. This is sunshine baking at its best and is guaranteed to impress those you love to cook for.

Serves 10 to 12

For the crust
1½ cups almonds
1⅓ cups pecans
⅔ cup pistachios
1 cup dried apricots softened in hot water, or soft medjool dates, pits removed, or a mix of both
¼ teaspoon of salt

For the filling
Generous 1 pound fresh apricots, pits removed, 8 ounces sliced
½ cup almond butter (see page 13)
¼ cup maple syrup, plus 2 tablespoons for topping
1 heaped teaspoon vanilla bean paste or extract
Zest of ½ orange
1 tablespoon almond or coconut oil, melted
⅓ cup pistachios, ground

1. Preheat the oven to 350°F. Grease and line a 9-inch tart pan.

2. Put all the ingredients for the crust into a food-processor and blitz until combined. Evenly spread the crust around the base and up the sides of the prepared pan, using your hands or the back of a spoon to smooth it out.

3. Put the whole pitted apricots into a food-processor and blend to a purée, then add the almond butter, ¼ cup maple syrup, vanilla bean paste, and half the orange zest and blitz until combined. Spread the mixture on top of the crust.

4. Arrange the apricot slices in neat rings on top of the filling. Mix together the remaining maple syrup and orange zest with the almond or coconut oil, then brush this glaze over the apricots. Bake for 25 minutes, or until the filling and the apricots are golden.

5. Before serving, sprinkle over the ground pistachios and drizzle over some more orange maple glaze if you wish.

MAPLE PECAN
MOCHA PIE *VEGETARIAN

This irresistible dessert classic is given an inspired mocha twist, adding to its heavenly combination of rich toasted nuttiness and caramel sweetness. My pastry enriched with pecans is an ideal shortcut when time is not on your side and creates an added depth of nutty charm. A spoonful of crème fraîche is an ideal accompaniment here. One slice might just not be enough!

Serves 10 to 12

12 to 14-ounce package store-bought pie crust
2⅔ cups pecans, finely ground

For the filling
2⅔ cups pecans, roughly chopped
⅔ cup maple syrup
3 tablespoons unsalted butter
3 tablespoons crunchy maple peanut or honey cinnamon cashew butter (or crunchy peanut butter)
6 tablespoons heavy cream
¼ cup soft brown sugar
1 tablespoon instant coffee granules dissolved in 2 tablespoons hot water
1 tablespoon raw cacao (or 100% cocoa) powder
5 egg yolks
1 teaspoon vanilla bean paste or extract
1 teaspoon freshly grated nutmeg
Pinch of salt

1. Preheat the oven to 400°F. Unroll the sheet of pie crust and sprinkle the finely ground pecans evenly all over the surface. Roll up the pastry from one end to the other into a long round sausage shape, then bring together into a ball and knead with your fingers until the pecans are distributed throughout. On a lightly floured surface, roll out the pastry and use to line a 9-inch-diameter, 2-inch-deep tart pan with a removable base. Prick the base with a fork and chill for 20 minutes.

2. Meanwhile, spread the pecans over a baking tray and cook in the oven for 5 to 7 minutes, or until lightly toasted. Remove and set aside.

3. Line the chilled pastry shell with parchment paper and then pie weights or beans. Bake for 15 minutes on a baking sheet, then remove the weights and paper,

and return the pastry shell to the oven for a further 5 minutes, or until the pastry is lightly golden. Remove and reduce the oven temperature to 350°F.

4. Put the maple syrup, both butters, cream, sugar, coffee, and cacao powder in a pan and warm briefly over a low heat until the butters have melted and the sugar has dissolved. Leave to cool slightly.

5. Beat the egg yolks in a bowl, then stir in the slightly cooled syrup mixture, the pecans, vanilla, nutmeg, and a pinch of salt. Pour the mixture into the pastry case and bake for 30 minutes, or until set. Serve warm or cold with crème fraîche or ice cream, if you wish.

CHOPPED
& WHOLE

MAPLE-ROASTED NUT & SEED GRANOLA
*VEGETARIAN

Homemade granola is one of the easiest, most satisfying things to make. For me, it's one of those any-time-of-day foods and I love to whip up a batch on a Sunday evening and use it throughout the week. (It will keep for up to a month stored in an airtight container.)

Serves 6

1 cup rolled oats
⅓ cup each pecans, Brazil nuts, hazelnuts, and walnuts, roughly chopped (or use a mix of any nuts)
3 tablespoons mixed small seeds (e.g. hemp, linseed, chia, sesame)
1½ tablespoons each pumpkin seeds and sunflower seeds
1 teaspoon pie spice
½ teaspoon cinnamon
⅓ cup maple syrup

For the blueberrry compote
1 cup blueberries
2 tablespoons maple syrup
Squeeze of lime juice

To serve
2 cups plain or Greek yogurt
Fresh blueberries and blackberries
Maple syrup

1. Preheat the oven to 400°F and line a baking sheet with parchment paper.

2. Combine the oats, nuts, and seeds in a bowl with the spices, then pour over the maple syrup and stir to coat. Spread out evenly onto the baking sheet and bake for 8 to 10 minutes, or until golden and toasted. Remove and set aside to cool completely.

3. For the blueberry compote, place all the ingredients into a small pan and bring to the boil. Reduce the heat to low and gently simmer for 3 to 4 minutes, or until thickened. Add a tablespoon of water if it becomes too thick.

4. To serve, spoon some yogurt into the bowls, divide the granola and the compote on top. Finish with some fresh blueberries and blackberries and a drizzle of maple syrup.

Oats deliver impressive amounts of fiber and iron, while the nuts and seeds add heart-healthy, unsaturated fats, slow energy-release protein and brain-boosting B vitamins.

NUTTY ANCHOÏADE & GRILLED VEGETABLES

*GLUTEN-FREE *DAIRY-FREE

This Mediterranean-influenced nutty, garlicky sauce is a culinary delight. Its flavor enhances the grilled vegetables perfectly, making this a superb simple starter or light lunch. You can make it in a mortar and pestle if you prefer—the texture is half the pleasure of this chunky dip—otherwise pulse briefly in a food-processor or blender.

Serves 4

For the anchoïade
½ teaspoon cumin seeds
⅓ cup chopped almonds
⅓ cup chopped walnuts
1 large garlic clove, peeled
4 to 5 good quality anchovy fillets in oil, drained
A handful of fresh flat-leaf parsley
Zest and juice of 1 lime
2 teaspoons red wine vinegar
⅓ cup–6 tablespoons walnut oil (or good-quality extra-virgin olive oil)

For the vegetables
1 large zucchini, cut into bite-sized chunks
4 to 6 asparagus spears
1 red pepper, sliced into thick strips
3 baby eggplants, sliced into thick strips
½ cup vine cherry tomatoes
Olive oil, for frying
Salt

1. Begin by making the anchoïade. Toast the cumin seeds in a dry frying pan for a few minutes, until fragrant, then grind to a fine powder in a blender or using a mortar and pestle.

2. Add the nuts, garlic, lime zest, and juice, anchovies, parsley, and red wine vinegar, continuing to pulse until the nuts are finely chopped, but still chunky. Finally, add the oil, pouring in a steady stream with the motor still running, until you achieve the desired consistency.

3. Heat some olive oil in a large grill pan, and cook the vegetables for five minutes, or until charred. Add a sprinkle of salt and serve with the anchoïade.

SATAY STEAK WITH CUCUMBER RIBBONS

*DAIRY-FREE

Bring a little sweet and spice to your oven (or barbecue) with these juicy steak skewers served with lashings of spicy satay sauce, cool cucumber strips, and salty peanuts. *Kecap manis* is a sticky and sweet soy sauce from the international section of the supermarket. Taste satays-faction guaranteed!

*Serves 2 as main or
4 as a starter
(You will need 4 wooden
skewers, soaked in water)*

14-ounce rib-eye steak, chopped into bite-sized chunks

For the satay sauce
1 large garlic clove
1 to 2 red chiles, halved and deseeded
½ stem of lemongrass
1-inch piece of fresh ginger, roughly chopped
1 teaspoon ground cumin
1 teaspoon ground coriander
2 tablespoons *kecap manis*
1 tablespoon each soy sauce and toasted sesame oil
½ tablespoon fish sauce
Zest and juice of ½ lime
½ cup crunchy peanut butter
¼ cup coconut milk, plus extra

To serve
½ cucumber
¼ cup salted peanuts
A handful of cilantro
1 lime, cut into wedges

1. Put the garlic, chiles, lemongrass, and ginger into a small food-processor and whizz until finely chopped. Place into a large bowl and stir in the remaining satay sauce ingredients except the coconut milk. Transfer half of the mixture into a bowl, add the steak and stir to evenly coat. Set aside until needed.

2. Put the remaining satay mixture into a saucepan with the coconut milk and heat gently while stirring, until the sauce is warmed through and begins to darken a little. Add more coconut milk or water if you need to: you want a smooth, dipping consistency.

3. Preheat the broiler of the oven. Evenly thread the steak onto the skewers and place onto a lightly oiled baking sheet. Cook for 6 to 8 minutes, turning occasionally, until charred on the edges and cooked to your liking.

4. Using a peeler or mandoline, peel long strips from the cucumber, then roughly chop the salted peanuts.

5. Serve the skewers with the cucumber ribbons, peanuts, cilantro, and lime wedges and the satay sauce for dipping.

TURMERIC WALNUTS & CHICORY SALAD

*VEGETARIAN *GLUTEN-FREE *DAIRY-FREE

The stars of the show here are my sticky turmeric walnuts, which add a fiery punch to this fresh and zesty salad. Turmeric has long-revered powerful anti-inflammatory and antioxidant effects, making this an all-round superfood crowd-winner, which will take pride of place at your table.

Serves 4

For the walnuts
⅓ cup honey
½ teaspoon ground turmeric
Pinch of chile flakes
Pinch of sea salt
1 cup walnuts

For the salad
2 lemons, halved lengthwise, seeds removed, and sliced into thin segments
2 tablespoons walnut oil (or other)
4 endives, outer leaves removed and inner core sliced into quarters
1 cup pea shoots or watercress
½ cup fresh fava beans, blanched
A handful of fresh oregano leaves
Salt and pepper

1. Preheat the oven to 350°F. Put the honey, turmeric, chile flakes, and salt into a small bowl and whisk to combine. You should have a thick paste; add a little water to loosen if necessary. Add the walnuts and stir so they are well coated. Spread the mixture out onto a lined baking tray and roast for 15 to 20 minutes, or until golden but still a little sticky. Remove from the oven and set aside until needed.

2. Increase the temperature of the oven to 400°F. Bring a small pan of water to the boil, then add the lemon wedges and blanch for a few minutes. Transfer to a large ovenproof dish or roasting pan and spread out in a single layer. Drizzle over the oil and a sprinkling of salt, then roast in the oven for 15 minutes, or until the lemon slices have started to turn golden and charred at the edges.

3. Add the endives, and a little more oil if needed, and cook for a further 5 minutes. Remove from the oven and allow to cool.

4. To serve, toss the pea shoots through the lemon and endive, then scatter over the walnuts, fava beans, and oregano. Finish with a little salt and freshly ground black pepper.

ROASTED EGGPLANT WITH DUKKAH

*VEGETARIAN *GLUTEN-FREE

An upgrade from your typical roasted veg, this guaranteed crowd-pleaser is perfect as a tasty appetizer to begin the meal or served as a gratifying side dish. This is vegan comfort food at its best—and healthy too. The eggplant's delicate smoky flavor positively sings when topped with ricotta, artichoke, and tomato, and the dukkah adds a wonderful nutty charm and sweet layer of crunch. Dukkah (pronounced "Doo-kah") is an aromatic Egyptian spice blend made from various roasted nuts, seeds, and spices.

Serves 2 to 4

2 eggplants, halved
  lengthways
Hemp seed (or other) oil,
  for drizzling
1 cup cherry tomatoes,
  quartered
2 garlic cloves, finely
  chopped
4 ounces canned artichoke
  hearts, drained and sliced
  (about 12 slices)
½ cup ricotta
2 tablespoons dukkah
¼ cup hazelnuts, roughly
  chopped
A few sprigs of fresh thyme
Salt and pepper

1. Preheat the oven to 400°F. Using a sharp knife, criss-cross the flesh side of the halved eggplants. Transfer to a baking pan and brush liberally with hemp seed oil and season with salt and pepper. Bake for 20 minutes, or until the flesh begins to soften and turn golden. Remove from the oven and set aside until needed.

2. Mix together the tomatoes and garlic with a little more seasoning in a bowl and spoon over the eggplant flesh. Divide the artichoke and ricotta over the top, then sprinkle over the dukkah and hazelnuts. Drizzle with a little more oil then return to the oven and bake for a further 15 minutes. Before serving, add a few sprigs of thyme.

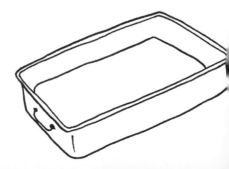

CASHEW CAESAR SALAD & SHRIMP

A gentle twist on the Mexican classic, this gorgeous salad is full of fresh, satisfying flavors. With the addition of my rich cashew nut Caesar dressing, it is also rich in B vitamins—essential for a healthy brain and heart—boosting the nutritional value of this dish.

Serves 2

For the dressing
⅓ cup raw cashews, soaked for 2 to 3 hours (or preferably overnight)
4 good-quality anchovy fillets in oil, drained
A good squeeze of lemon juice
1 tablespoon Dijon mustard
1 tablespoon tahini paste
2 teaspoons Worcestershire sauce
1 teaspoon garlic powder
⅓ cup canola (or olive) oil
3 tablespoons cashew or almond milk

1 tablespoon canola oil
1 garlic clove, crushed
7 ounces raw large shrimp, peeled
3 slices of pancetta
3 heads little gem lettuce
½ cup fine green beans, cooked
A small handful of chopped chives
2 soft boiled eggs, halved
¼ cup Parmesan shavings
¼ cup toasted cashews, chopped
Salt and pepper

1. For the dressing, drain and rinse the cashews, then put all the ingredients except the oil and nut milk into a food-processor or blender and blitz until smooth. With the motor still running, gradually add the oil, then the nut milk, until you achieve a creamy dressing. Season to taste with salt and pepper.

2. Heat the canola oil in a pan, then add the garlic and shrimp with a little salt and pepper. Cook for 5 to 6 minutes, or until the shrimp are pink, cooked through, and lightly golden. Remove from the pan and set aside. Add the pancetta and cook until crisp. When cool enough to handle, break into pieces.

3. When you are ready to serve, separate the the lettuce leaves and place in a large bowl with the beans, shrimp, pancetta and chives, drizzle with 3 tablespoons of the dressing and toss to combine. Divide the salad between two plates and top with the egg. Scatter over the Parmesan shavings and toasted cashews and serve with extra dressing on the side. Any leftover dressing will keep stored in an airtight container in the fridge for up to 2 weeks.

To make this dairy-free, omit the Parmesan. If you don't have garlic powder, substitute with 1 crushed garlic clove.

SUNFLOWER, RHUBARB & MACKEREL SALAD

*GLUTEN-FREE *DAIRY-FREE

The sharp, fruity accompaniment of rhubarb in this salad pairs brilliantly with oily fish such as the peppered mackerel used here, cutting through its rich flavor. The sunflower seeds add a wonderful crunch to every bite, making this salad not only tasty, but nutritionally balanced too. Bring on lunch!

Serves 2

2 tablespoons honey
1 long stem of rhubarb, trimmed and sliced on the diagonal
2 cups baby leaf kale
6 ounces peppered mackerel, torn into small pieces
¼ cup edamame beans, cooked as per package instructions
¼ cup sunflower seeds
A small handful of mint leaves, large leaves torn
Pumpkin seed (or other) oil
1 × container store-bought edamame bean hummus (alternatively you can use any variety hummus you like; beet hummus works just as well)

1. Heat ⅔ cup water and the honey in a medium-sized pan, stirring until the honey dissolves. Add the rhubarb and simmer for about 5 minutes, until just tender but still intact (be careful to not overcook). Use a slotted spoon to remove the rhubarb and transfer to a plate to cool completely.

2. When you are ready to serve, divide the baby kale, mackerel, rhubarb, and edamame beans between two plates. Scatter over the sunflower seeds and mint leaves and drizzle with pumpkin seed oil. Season with salt and freshly ground black pepper. Serve with the edamame hummus on the side.

HOT-SMOKED SALMON & SPELT SALAD

Spelt is an ancient whole grain that has a wonderful al dente quality. I use it a lot in salads as it has a satisfying earthy, nutty texture and is very versatile. Spelt's distant cousins, farro and barley, would also work well here. The yogurt and mint dressing can be made in a flash and adds a fresh, minty zing to the flavorsome hot-smoked salmon.

Serves 2

1 medium zucchini, spiralized (or sliced into very fine julienne)
4-6 spears asparagus
½ cup pea shoots
¼ cup garden peas, cooked
½ cup spelt, cooked according to package instructions
6 ounces hot-smoked salmon
1 tablespoon mixed pumpkin, sunflower, and linseeds
A few mint leaves, to serve
Pumpkin seed (or other) oil, for drizzling
Salt and pepper

For the yogurt and mint dip
½ cup plain or Greek yogurt
Zest of ½ lemon
3 to 4 large mint leaves, roughly chopped

1. Blanch the zucchini "pasta" and asparagus in boiling water for about 5 minutes, until soft but with still a bit of bite, then remove and run under cold water.

2. For the dip, mix together the yogurt, lemon zest, and mint, and season to taste.

3. To serve, arrange the pea shoots, zucchini, peas, asparagus, and spelt onto two plates, then top with the hot-smoked salmon and a sprinkling of seeds. Finish with a few mint leaves, some seasoning, and a drizzle of pumpkin seed oil. Serve with the yogurt and mint dip on the side.

VIETNAMESE PORK WITH TAHINI
*DAIRY-FREE

All the spicy, sweet, salty, and sour vibrant flavors of Vietnam packed into one delicious curry for you to enjoy at home. I add tahini for a quick calcium boost and top with crunchy peanuts and sesame seeds for the ultimate balance of textures, creating the perfect finish to every mouthful.

Serves 2

10 ounces pork tenderloin fillet, sliced into 6 medallions
2 tablespoons honey
1 tablespoon *kecap manis* (or dark soy sauce)
1 tablespoon tahini
1 tablespoon sesame seed oil
1 spring onion, sliced
1 garlic clove, finely chopped
1 thumb-sized piece of fresh ginger, grated
1 large red chile, seeded and finely chopped
1 stem of lemongrass, outer leaf removed, finely chopped
½ cup sugar snap peas
2 bok choy, leaves separated
1 red pepper, sliced
1 tablespoon fish sauce
Squeeze of lime
¾ cup coconut milk
Black pepper

To serve
3½ ounces udon noodles
¼ cup salted peanuts
2 teaspoons sesame seeds
Thai basil or cilantro

1. Put the pork slices in a bowl with the honey, *kecap manis* (or dark soy sauce) and tahini. Turn the pork to coat it, cover and leave to marinate for 30 minutes–2 hours.

2. Heat the oil in a large, deep non-stick pan. Remove the pork from the marinade, reserving the marinade, and cook for 2 minutes on each side, or until charred all over. Transfer to a plate.

3. Reduce the heat and add the spring onion, garlic, ginger, chile, and lemongrass (with a little more oil if needed). Gently cook for 5 to 6 minutes until softened.

4. Return the pork to the pan, along with the reserved marinade and the sugar snap peas, bok choy, and red pepper, and fry for another minute. Season with the fish sauce, a squeeze of lime and some freshly ground black pepper. Add the coconut milk and bring to the boil, then reduce the temperature and simmer gently for 10 minutes.

5. Meanwhile, cook the noodles according to the package instructions and roughly chop the peanuts.

6. Toss the curry with the noodles and serve with chopped peanuts, a sprinkling of sesame seeds, a handful of fresh Thai basil or cilantro leaves, and extra chile and lime wedges, if you wish.

TAHINI & MISO CAULIFLOWER STEAKS

*VEGETARIAN *DAIRY-FREE

Transform the humble cauliflower into a modern marvel and let these blooming beauties stand proud. These versatile crumbly white florets and tender stems now epitomize vegetable royalty. This dish captures all that is right about the marriage of wonderful flavors indigenous to Middle Eastern cuisine. A word of warning, however: it's highly addictive!

Serves 4

1 large cauliflower head, sliced into steaks (inner leaves separated and outer leaves discarded)
1 tablespoon canola or olive oil, plus extra
1 garlic clove, crushed
1 tablespoon white miso paste
1 tablespoon tahini paste
2 teaspoons rice wine vinegar
1 teaspoon black or white sesame seeds
A handful of fresh mint leaves, roughly chopped
Salt and pepper

1. Preheat the oven to 400°F. Place the cauliflower and leaves, spaced apart, on a roasting pan (you may need two).

2. In a bowl, mix together the oil, garlic, miso paste, tahini paste, rice vinegar, and some seasoning, then use a pastry brush to generously coat the cauliflower until evenly covered. Drizzle generously with some extra oil.

3. Roast for 20 minutes, or until the cauliflower is tender, golden, and the leaves are crisp. Remove from the oven and allow to cool slightly.

4. Before serving, sprinkle over the sesame seeds and fresh mint.

These cauliflower steaks pair brilliantly with any grilled meats, especially lamb.

LABNEH & SUMAC WITH ZUCCHINI

Labneh is yogurt that has been strained to remove its whey, resulting in a thicker consistency than unstrained yogurt while preserving its distinctive, sour taste. The vibrant Middle Eastern spice sumac has a mild, almost lemony flavor. It's available at most large supermarkets. The dish can be prepared in very little time—which, for something so nutritious and flavorsome, is no mean feat.

Serves 6 to 8

1½ cups labneh (I use Lebanese style)
Zest of ½ lemon
1 tablespoon pistachios, toasted and chopped
1 tablespoon slivered or whole almonds, toasted and chopped
A small handful of cilantro, roughly chopped (optional)
Pinch of sumac
1½ tablespoons canola, almond, or good-quality olive oil
1 zucchini, cut with a peeler lengthwise into ribbons
Grilled flatbread, to serve
Salt and pepper

1. Mix the labneh with the lemon zest and salt and pepper to taste and place in a dish. Scatter the surface with the nuts, chopped cilantro, if using, and sumac, then drizzle with oil.

2. Serve the labneh with the zucchini, drizzled with a little more oil, and the flatbread on the side.

HALLOUMI & ALMOND TACOS *VEGETARIAN

Taco heaven is created here with the combination of sweet peppers, creamy avocado, salty, textured halloumi, spicy chile, and wonderfully crunchy almonds. These fresh-tasting, punchy tacos go particularly well with the creamy consistency of my homemade almond sauce. Feel free to add more chile, or harissa, if you like things a little more spicy.

Makes 4 tacos

For the almond sauce
1 cup blanched almonds, soaked for at least 4 hours (or preferably overnight)
Zest and juice of 1 lime
1 teaspoon cumin
½ teaspoon chili powder
2 garlic cloves
1 large chile, seeded, plus extra, chopped, to serve
¾ cup plus 2 tablespoons almond milk (see page 12)
Salt and pepper

For the tacos
Almond or canola oil
1 red pepper, sliced lengthwise
8 ounces halloumi, cut into ¼-inch slices
1 large avocado
1 red chile, finely chopped
Squeeze of lime juice
4 mini soft flour tortillas
Handful of arugula leaves
Salt and pepper
1 tablespoon slivered almonds, toasted, to serve

1. For the almond sauce, drain and rinse the almonds, then blend all the ingredients together until smooth. Season to taste, then set aside until needed. (This makes more than you'll need, but will keep in the fridge for a week and works with just about anything grilled or savory.)

2. Heat a little oil in a pan, and briefly fry the pepper until it just begins to soften—it should still have some bite. Remove, then cook the halloumi on both sides until charred, adding more oil to the pan if needed.

3. In a small bowl, mash up the avocado roughly with a fork, then season and mix in the chile and lime juice and spread over the surface of the tortillas. (Heat these in the microwave for 30 seconds first if you wish.) Divide the arugula leaves, red pepper strips, and halloumi between each one and season with salt and freshly ground black pepper.

4. Serve garnished with the almonds and some more chopped chile if you wish. Drizzle with the almond sauce and serve with extra lime wedges, if you like. Alternatively, you can serve the tortillas with bowls of all the filling ingredients and sauce for everyone to make their own!

If you don't have time to soak the almonds, you can use ½ cup almond butter instead (reduce the almond milk to ½ cup).

FIGS WITH WHIPPED FETA

With their honeyed sweetness and delicate perfume, soft, purple-skinned figs are celebrated in this recipe. They are the perfect companions to salty, creamy whipped feta. The jewel-like pomegranate seeds offer a little burst of fruity flavor and the vibrant chopped pistachio adds interest and balance. Serve this on wholesome sunflower seed bread, drizzled with honey, and you have a simple, quick, and delicious light snack or informal dessert.

Serves 2 to 4

4 ounces feta
⅓ cup Greek yogurt
4 slices of sunflower seed
   bread (or rye bread)
4 ripe figs, sliced
2 tablespoons pomegranate
   seeds
2 tablespoons pistachios,
   roughly chopped
2 tablespoons honey

1. Using an electric mixer, whisk the feta until smooth, then stir in the Greek yogurt to combine.

2. Toast the sunflower seed bread, then spread each slice with the whipped feta.

3. Top with the figs and the pomegranate seeds and finish with a scattering of pistachios and a drizzle of honey.

PISTACHIO, CINNAMON & YOGURT BARK

*VEGETARIAN *GLUTEN-FREE

This incredibly simple dessert is the perfect palate cleanser finale to a summertime meal. The secret is to take it out of the freezer ahead of time—that way it will be lovely and soft. The fragrant roasted berries can be made ahead and warmed through before serving alongside. This recipe is made extra special thanks to the addition of earthy spices, which delicately balance the sweetness of these sumptuous and completely irresistible iced treats.

Serves 6 to 8

2 cups Greek yogurt
3 tablespoons date syrup
½ teaspoon each ground cinnamon and pie spice
1 tablespoon vanilla bean paste or extract
½ cup each fresh raspberries and blackberries
½ cup dried cranberries
1 tablespoon cacao nibs
⅔ cup pistachios, chopped, plus extra to serve

For the roasted berries
1 cup strawberries, halved and quartered
¾ cup each raspberries and blackberries
1 tablespoon vanilla bean paste or extract
2 tablespoons date syrup
½ tablespoon flaxseed oil

1. Line and grease an 8-inch square baking pan. In a bowl, stir together the yogurt, date syrup, spices, and vanilla. Gently stir in the fruit, cacao nibs, and ⅓ cup of the pistachios. Pour the mixture into the pan, spreading it out evenly, making sure the fruit and nuts are distributed throughout. Sprinkle the remaining pistachios over the surface, cover with plastic wrap and place in the freezer for 4 hours, or preferably overnight.

2. For the roasted berries, pre-heat the oven to 350°F. Place the berries in a baking dish and spread out in an even layer.

3. In a small bowl, mix together the vanilla, date syrup, and oil with 1 tablespoon of water. Pour the mixture over the fruit and roast in the oven for 20 minutes, or until the berries are tender and caramelized. Remove from the oven and allow to cool.

4. Remove the baking pan from the freezer and run the outside under hot water for 10 seconds before gently releasing the frozen yogurt "bark." Set aside for 10 minutes or until it has slightly softened, then use a serrated knife to slice it into equal lengths.

5. Scatter with a few more chopped pistachios and serve with the roasted berries.

INDEX

NOTES ON BRANDS

Here are some of my favorites for more unusual ingredients:

Nut and coconut flours
Bob's Red Mill (available in Whole Foods Markets and many supermarkets).
www.bobsredmill.com

Coconut and nut oils
Spectrum (available in many supermarkets).
www.spectrumorganics.com

Milled flax, chia seed, apple & cinnamon
Linwoods (available in Whole Foods Markets, The Fresh Market, H-E-B and online).
www.linwoodshealthfoods.com

Nut and seed butters
Meridian and Pip & Nut (available from some large supermarkets and online).
www.meridianfoods.co.uk
www.pipandnut.co.uk

ACKNOWLEDGMENTS

Writing and styling this book has been a thrilling voyage of discovery and I am so grateful to the many people who have helped see it through from beginning to end. This was an exploration of exciting new waters, and thanks to the talented and passionate group of people that joined me, the venture has been both fun, fruitful, and what you might call an act of self-belief, love, and determination.

To the wonderful team at Kyle Books, specifically Judith Hannam who made my dream a reality, my superb editor Claire Rogers, whose support, guidance, and "voice of calm" throughout has been paramount, and all the passionate people they brought in to work on this project with me.

To Jacqui Melville, your innate ability to seek out additional props assisted in more ways than you can imagine. Thank you for truly understanding my sentiment. To the brilliant Faith Mason for helping create my vision while capturing all that is fresh and delicious and Jenni Desmond for the illustrative work which I believe adds so much in all its detailed and delicate glory; I'm so thrilled you all came along for the ride, you are in some way apart of this book forever more.

Special thanks must also go to the brilliant and beautiful people I am lucky enough to call my friends and family. Some of whom volunteered as my enthusiastic and willing panel of taste testers. (Tough gig, I know!) You have all kept me smiling and sane throughout the whole process. It's impossible to list each and everyone of you but you know who you are and how exceptionally grateful I am. There is however one very special lady I wish to mention; my mama Julie. You have been my biggest inspiration of all and in spite of everything, my rock. I would have been at a loss without all your love, honesty, and unwavering support.

And of course to everyone who has bought my first book—after all, you are the reason this was created! I hope you reap enjoyment from all the passion and dedicated spirit that filled every page and embrace just how simple it can be to create tempting, nourishing, and well-balanced meals full of harmonious flavors for everyday eating. We are all joy seekers, so let's get in the kitchen, cook happy and enjoy the fruits of our labor.

Published in 2017 by Kyle Books
www.kylebooks.com

Distributed by National Book Network
4501 Forbes Blvd, Suite 200,
Lanham, MD 20706
Phone: (800) 462-6420
Fax: (800) 338-4550
customercare@nbnbooks.com

First published in Great Britain in 2017 by
Kyle Books, an imprint of Kyle Cathie Ltd

10 9 8 7 6 5 4 3 2 1

ISBN 978 1 909487 70 3

Project Editor: Claire Rogers
Copy Editor: Anne McDowall
Designer: Helen Bratby
Photographer: Faith Mason
Illustrator: Jenni Desmond
Food Stylist: Natalie Seldon
Prop Stylist: Natalie Seldon and
    Jacqui Melville
Production: Nic Jones and Gemma John

Library of Congress Control Number:
2016958798

Color reproduction by ALTA London
Printed and bound in China by C&C Offset
Printing Co., Ltd.

* Note: all eggs are free-range